The Pink House of

Purple Yam Preserves

& Other Poems

The Pink House of
Purple Yam Preserves
& Other Poems

with my very best regards,
Aileen

Aileen I. Cassinetto

Our Own Voice & Little Dove Books, 2018

OUR OWN VOICE
Arlington, VA
www.oovrag.com

LITTLE DOVE BOOKS
Morgan Hill, CA
littledovebooks.wordpress.com

CONTENTS

Selected Poems

From "The Enormous River Encircling the World"

In ocean-speak,
learn the art of camouflage.

That sound you hear—ambient noise, they call it—is really
Okeanos' dragon tail swirling, whorl-like, with "all

the might of the ocean stream."
Best take your cue from the Nautilus (pelagic and unchanged),

or the Sailfin sculpin (eye-banded and demersal),
or the Leafy seadragon (which, in captivity, is unbreedable).

But beware
the Angelfish and the Butterfly splitfin.

Listen:
Regard with wonder the Weedy seadragon on their rocky reefs,

and the Longsnout seahorse on coral reefs.
Also Janss' pipefish and his unparalleled brood pouch,

and Shaw's cowfish: carapace-cased, rough-water warriors.
Discover the blue-emitting Brittle star, and the Sunfish in its wholeness,

the Sea pink coastliners and the lovely Seaside fleabane, also pink.
There's the beach sagebrush—silver and salt-washed.

Above all,
find the Dwarf cuttlefish, masters of camouflage—

stumpy-spined Indo-Pacific survivors,
they've actually learned to "walk."

Best be like a cuttle, ambling flamboyantly...
dangerously.

Isle of Skye, 1920

The whole thing changed.
The lighthouse in eclipsed
light and the line
of the coast, dissolving
like salt
cellars on a lace tablecloth,
only the Jackmanii
remained, wedge-shaped—
purple and unresolved.
As for the kitchen table—
there it was, scoured and
upended in the fork
of a pear tree, its four legs
in the air, like a Chinese road
painting, liquescing into a blank
canvas, white and unwavering.

Point Joe

Understand how an old sailor
misread these rocks
and the force beneath motions
of water and air.

Salt spray, in the wake of
undulating ferocities, yields
rust, fog, or in acts of scattering,
luminous flux.

He stood watch at the helm,
on course, steady.
Until the *Catalina* went down.

How do you mark less than shining hours?
The loss of a ship?
A limb?
Daughters.

In Monterey Bay, he understood it all—
the movement of waves and wind,
how they circle an ocean,
how they carry dust, droplets, fragments of bone.

Tea in the Sahara

Dear Aunt Therese who does not pour tea
nevertheless disconcerts—

Her cup full of sand,
she follows the Caravan Trail of Dates,

where, at a watering stop,
women with many colored wraps invite her to tea.

They steep the leaves and pour her a glass.
She tastes sweetness thrice infused with mint.

She offers them her cheek to kiss,
she sips again, then dips her scone.

Dear Aunt Therese, in twenty years,
has not poured tea.

She pretends not to care, even as the other
guests pretend she isn't there.

The Short Season Between Two Silences

At the convalescent home for
winter plums,

the sickest

trees
rarely
season. Too

survive the
wounded
and

misshapen

with
knots
around
limbs,
they
perish
steadily.
some,

monstrous

dead

In
the girdled
arms

have
grown

sideways
despairingly,
and

as though

in perpetuity,
reaching for the sun.

A Day at the Museum with a Poet

—for Eileen Tabios

All days should be like this:
blissful, unhurried and art-filled.

With two women and "The Beach at Trouville"—here's a
world hemmed in by parasols and flounces, grains of sand and
shell on its surface. Was that uncertainty in the summer of
1870?

Or impermanence, and the world abstracted and manifold in
Braque's sea and sky and in both sailboats in the spring of
1909. Such cubic oddities in the "Little Harbor in Normandy,"

and in "The Scallop Shell"—Picasso's 1912 oval still-life
embodying a tabletop (or flat canvas?) where pipe, seashells,
and the world coming apart came together, blazoning, "our
future is in the air."

"Sunflowers." Skyward and yellow. Faithful and yellow. Dear
heart. Vincent, Vincent! Were all your days like this? Blissful,
unhurried, joy-filled?

The Cabinet of the World and

the Journeys of Women

Caroline of Ansbach's cabinet of curiosities is probably the
    most famous in the world—
it held a 'unicorn horn' (*naturalia*),
bezoar stones (*mirabilia*),
an ivory box of gold dust (*artificialia*),
a gallery of portraits (*artefacta*),
and all the books ever written (*scientifica*).
But how do you catalog
ideas such as inoculation?
or "miniature shoes belonging to lost children"?
Or newer installations such as
a dress of sorrows,
or the journeys of women
journaled,
or mapped on cloth.
Surely, these must be classified
apart from items wrested
from nature or wrought by man;
surely, it warrants its own class—
one that speaks of grit and
mother wit. Like the secret
name of woman—*triumpha*,
which means undaunted, forever stronghearted.

House of Cider Press

Mantes, my pretty,
I missed my train to Giverny.

From steam and smoke, I rose
to reach the waterlily pond

where the Epte River marries the Seine.
I beseeched the pink pebbledash

and the wisteria walls to conceal
me, amongst the marigolds.

Perhaps the bellflowers?
Or the Blue Thistles?

Surely not the sweet peas,
nor the red hollyhocks.

Lo and behold, the Delphiniums
dragged their gaze southward,

and bid me catch a train
to Saint-Lazare. Risk the goblin

ore, and find
my true cobalt blue.

Last word is the poet's calling

—after Bill Moyers (Journal, 22 January 2010) and
Danielle Legros Georges ("Poem for the Poorest
Country In the Western Hemisphere" and "The
Yellow Forms of Paradise")

O
poorest country
in the Western

Hemisphere,
your daughter
Danielle called you

beacon
and flame,
the grandfather at

the
gate, with
the flashlight, with

the
crossroad light.
What would you

not
give for
an areito, sweet

music
of the
Tainos, of your

daughter,
Anacaona, Golden
Flower of your

people's
struggle. Liberty
or Death, swore

your
Generals, "paradise
suspended from their

necks
like a
giant clock." You

are
born of
Revolution and song,

and
the chant
goes on, while

your
daughters sew
dresses for eleven

cents
an hour.
Last word is

the
poet's calling.
"Oh poorest country,

this
is not
your name." You

were
beacon, and
therefore, light, shining,

beckoning
unfettered hearts
at the crossroads.

The Auction

Seen
here, the
white love seat

where
he slept
for nine years.

In the Island of Good Boots

> "One had to be groomed—by culture, by
> tradition, by authority—into servitude."
> —Ninotchka Rosca

Of course, kasama (companion)
sounds gentler, more
charitable, somehow, less
demeaning, even, when
compared to katulong (helper),
utusan (servant) or, heaven
forbid, alipin (slave)
—a word which hasn't been used
in over five decades—
Kikay/Emmy/Malou/Lourdes/
Betty/Alice/Gigi/Baby/
Fracing/Honey/Anali/Ming/
Puring/Nora/Lilia/Yaya—
Manang,
Pakibili ako ng _____.
(Please go to the store and buy me _____.)
Pakikuha yung _____.
(Please go fetch _____.)
Paki plantsa.
(Please iron.)
Paki—
is a gentler, somehow more
charitable, somehow less
demeaning version of utos (command).

"One had to be groomed—by culture, by tradition, by authority—" to be
a benevolent master.
Pakitali—
Please tie my shoes.

B & O Blues No. 3

"Go west, young man…"
As did the railroads before you. And the immigrants who built them.

By 1868, six years after passage of the Pacific Railway Act, more than 12,000 Chinese workers were employed by Central Pacific, laying ten miles of track a day, eastward (at $27 per month), blasting areas for track in the Sierra Nevada, and paying taxes without the right to citizenship.

The Union Pacific's Irish laborers, mostly veterans of the Union and Confederate armies, laid track westward at $35 per month.

At Promontory Summit in Utah on May 10, 1869—690 miles of track from Sacramento, and 1,087 from Omaha—the two railroads met.

The first route connecting the west coast to the east carried a shipment from the Far East to the Old West: Japanese teas.

Not long after, droves of new settlers came. From the Eastern Seaboard, they boarded trains that took them all the way to the Pacific.

San Francisco Haiku

From the Golden Gate Bridge,
a glimpse of what was golden
summer of '67

send me a postcard
of that City by the Bay
with gold in her hair

The Summer of Love

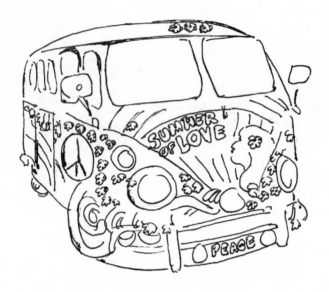

In the summer of 1967,
Something extraordinary happened in
    San Francisco.

Spurred by a sequence of events—
    the Fifties' conformism,
    the Cold War,
    the Vietnam War,
    the anti-war protests,
    the civil rights movement,
    the music of the Beatles and Bob Dylan,
    the poetry of Whitman's wild children—

100,000 young people
     —flowers in hair
     and barefooted,
     tie-dyed shirted,
     paisley-patterned skirted—

descended on Haight-Ashbury,
unravelling a cultural revolution
with "no political knowledge... yet [achieving]
    enormously political ends..."

The Promise

—for Carol & Erik

Take these symbols of love,
to be perfect and unbroken,

all ends joining
and curved, as though

yielding, for love
is unconditional, and marriage,

a compromise:
Gold-spun rings

to wear from this day forward,
morsels of cake

for good fortune,
tossed rice and tied knots

to honor our traditions,
friends and kinsmen and other well-wishers,

songs of love and poems of hope,
and you, fairest,

all the days of my life
I take you, faithfully,

and without reserve, as I say my oath
today, will you take me and mine,

in love, always, for love conquers
a multitude of wrongs,

as we live and breathe,
it gets sweeter, my sweet.

The Art of Salamat

"Taos pusong pasasalamat"—
   (Gracias, desde
      lo

más profundo de
   mi corazón) —
      must

then be prepositional,
   for it
      invokes

the heart, once
   believed to
      be

the seat of
   all affective
      states

of consciousness. To
   thank deeply,
      and

sincerely, (that is,
   heartfully and
      prepositionally)

implies that there
is a
recipient,

a benefactor, and
a good
deed

done. (Very different
from propositional
gratitude,

which merely suggests
a recipient's
appreciation

for a general
state of
affairs,

such as freedom
from want,
or

the absence of
rain on
a

given day.) To
    thank someone
        in

Filipino is to
    say, "Salamat"
        (most

likely Arabic in
    origin, for
        the

Arabs frequented a
    precolonial Philippines
        via

ancient trade routes).
    To use
        the

Filipino's language of
    gratitude is
        to

carry the heft
    of a
        sacred

duty. For every
    Filipino is
        aware

that "utang na
      loob" is
            a

debt that can
      never be
            entirely,

truly settled. This
      means, the
            beneficiary

is also, in
      equal measure,
            trustee—

keeper of the
      obligations of
            gratitude,

and honorable enough
      to repay
            a

favor (or pay
      it forward).
            In

other words, *marunong*
      tumanaw ng
            utang

na loob. Whether
    every act
        of

beneficence calls for
    some degree
        of

goodwill is debatable.
    "After 337
        days

holding out against
    soldiers of
        the

Katipunan, the small
    Spanish detachment,
        (barricaded

inside Baler's fortress-
    like church)
        finally

surrendered. In an
    act of
        benevolence,

President Emilio Aguinaldo,
    in 1899,
        decreed

that 'the survivors
        shall be
                treated

as friends not
        as prisoners.'"
                100

years later, in
        an equally
                "momentous

gesture, Spain's Congreso
        de Diputados
                formally

expressed the country's
        gratitude toward
                the

Philippines for declaring
        the Philippine-
                Spanish

Friendship Day on
        June 30
                of

every year in
        commemoration of
                the

historic Siege of
Baler. Spain's
unprecedented

move was made
in response
to

an equally unprecedented
initiative by
the

Philippines to pass
Republic Act
9187..."

For this and
other acts
of

beneficence, descendants of
the Spanish
soldiers

continue to bespeak
gestures of
goodwill—

the Philippine flag
flying in
perpetuity

in someone's ancestral
    home somewhere
        on

the Iberian peninsula.
    Or snatches
        of

lengua castellano afloat
    some island
        on

the Philippine archipelago.
    Some days,
        gratitude

is a canvas
    funnel that
        restrains

movement; it may
    also be
        that

it is all
    that prevents
        you

from drifting too
    far too
        soon.

The Boatman's Book Spine Poetry

Be
My Romance
On the High Seas of Discovery

Tattered Boat
Blood Orange
In Ordinary Time

Cherry Blossoms in the Time of Earthquakes and Tsunami
Sleep in Me

Monstress
Miracle Fruit
Fourteen Love Stories

Ode to the Heart Smaller than a Pencil Eraser
The Darker Fall

Disturbance
The Word on Paradise

Salambao

There we are in a spoon
full of water,
an oceanographer tells me.
Fishes, eyes, fish-eyes and I.
But what do I know
of waters? I am terribly
terrestrial in my thinking.
So terribly
finite on a raft.
A three hundred-year-old
fish would have more
wisdom. I wish
to write of waters
in remembrance of my mythic
forefather, island-man fisherman,
rowing two thousand
nautical miles without
a compass,
to cast out his net below
sunlit surface waters.
But here I am,
a century late,
with an orange
roughy on my plate.

Rooted

—A Ducktail Haynaku

Not
my native
land, but here

I
pick up
my pen, wield

it,
lay it
down, from this

heart to this land.

22nd Sunday in Ordinary Time

—for Remé

i.

In a measure are intervals of silence as resonant as echoic
memories. Like two beats and semitones, shifting keys
invoking unshakeable things: ventanillas bearing witness to
the passage of slight winds; floral patterned cottons
savouring mango-scented skin; sounds riding in grooves
etched on paraffin.

ii.

These are my instants: a girl on her knees, vows between
finger ridges; small hands feeling the breath of a gingham
ribbon; uneven shoulders balancing ten pounds of fish and
ten gallons of sweat; *sobre las olas,* a finger was guided above
the first black key in a group of three; this morning
savouring what was unblemished [bright, full-bodied,
invigorating].

iii.

I collect water droplets to re-create what I had once seen
there: colours. Vermilion, myrtle, azure, orcein, a
provenanced desk, a marked chronograph and sacrificed
pinctada.

iv.

Love, like Paloma's Groove, rests uneasily inside a blue box.
Love, like lanceolate leaves, waits unmoving above the waterline.
The message card reads: fill, add, cut, remove, replenish, add,
keep. Aren't these instructions to prolong life? Love, too?
Unwrap surprises in organza.

Orange Jessamine Road

in summertime, is a chalk-drawn
  hopscotch court. Every face evoked is young
    and wraithlike, springing forth, wildcrafted—

hibiscus, mock orange, lemon grass;
  breadnut and black plum; star apple,
    sweetsop, rose apple. You,

most beautiful and most brave, leapt boldly
  towards your moon, marked
    with the rind of a fruit and

the incidental leaf, silvery,
  from a golden leaf tree. But then, you were tangled
    mid-air, between a rosy expanse

and your half-circle on the ground. You landed,
  outwardly unfazed, on a chalk-drawn line.
    Yesterday, I thought of you.

How in the days of your invincibility, I was
  invincible, too, felled only
    by whiteflies and afternoon naps.

I wondered if you ever found
  that rind of fruit,
    if you remembered to jump,

over mock oranges,
over star apples,
over your moon.

The Pink House of
Purple Yam Preserves

After traveling 5,000 miles across the Pacific, the flowers are now iced, arrayed and ensconced on the side aisles of Santa Monica Church. The 18th century wooden torchères, however, looked sad and whitewashed next to the antique altar rails (the mother of the bride had the original polychromy painted over, to the absolute horror of the bride's future father-in-law, owner of said lamps). On a bright note, owing perhaps to a little deviousness on the part of the bride, the green carpet had been laid out, replacing the red her mother had just inspected a few hours ago.

Months of orchestration led to this day. A cast of thousands had been "recruited" to work thousands of hours to make this, the supposed wedding of the century, possible—the whole town was transformed. The church had been refurbished; old houses were torn down and, in their place, Spanish colonial homes were constructed; carriages from Austria, horses from Morocco and truckloads of antique furniture were ordered and delivered. The main road had been adorned with bougainvillea flowers (schoolteachers, in lieu of lesson plans, were instructed to make Japanese crepe paper blooms which they fastened onto live plants positioned along the road leading to the church).

To complete the colonial motif, every costume owned by the Cultural Center had been brought in as official attire for the townspeople; for the wedding party, bespoke turn-of-the-century *barongs* and *ternos* had been commissioned.

The bride's Filipiniana wedding gown, crafted by an Italian designer, was adorned with pearls and diamonds. (In hindsight, her more refined taste possibly drove her to walk down the aisle on her father's arm holding only her diamond rosary, having "conveniently" forgotten the large bouquet and ivory fan her mother had handpicked.)

To secure the best crowd, two dozen flights had been chartered for the 5,000 guests, including the bride's sister who had her matron-of-honor dress made—posthaste—from pink pineapple silk placemats on her way to the church.

Allowing for inflation, the wedding cost the taxpayers an estimated USD30,000,000.00.

This is, evidently, a country where parents loved their children fiercely—the poor sold their blood to hospitals to buy food for their kids. And the wealthy? Remember the bride's sister? Well, a few years ago, her parents bought an 18th century Princeton estate so that she could attend college "more comfortably." If that's not love, what is?

This is also a country where one in every 400 women worked as a prostitute. Most will never live to be a bride.

Years from now, the bride in the story will have the unfortunate torchères restored, for such is the way of the wealthy—they gentrify and they bring back the former things. Her mother, in the way of iron butterflies, will forever demand what she thinks is due her children.

The day's deeds are almost done. I cannot help but feel the immense weight of my young daughters' futures. Even now,

Aileen, my firstborn, reads more than she should play. She does not smile as often as I would like. She is not as attached to me as I had hoped. But she is devoted to her sister whom she is only getting to know.

When I gave birth to my youngest child, the doctors informed me that her kidneys were not "normal." Most mothers brought home their babies within days of giving birth. My daughter and I would stay at the hospital for the next few years—hoping for a cure, a lull, a miracle. I would not leave her side. Like I said, we tend to love our children fiercely.

When we finally came home five years later, the whole house had been repainted pink to welcome my five-year-old daughter. It took awhile to acclimate, but once we got settled, I started giving Aileen piano lessons. I taught her to play *Sobre Las Olas*—"Over the Waves"—for it is lovely and sweet, which is what I secretly hoped her future would be. And sometimes, she would hug me quickly, spontaneously, before turning away.

Tomorrow is Sunday, the 12th—Independence Day in a country that is still very much under military rule. Today's deeds are done. But there is a great deal to do around the house for it is an old house and requires much care. Already, my purple yam vines seem to be overtaking the whole place! I need to prune them back. Burn the bulbils.

Years ago, I dug out the roots of my bougainvillea plants for while stunning, they were mostly ornamental and had thorns which could have easily caused injury. I chose to grow purple yam instead. Sophia, my youngest, could live on *ube* if I let her.

A tender perennial, I find this root vegetable to be very resilient. The few bulbils I planted around a trellis have grown vigorously, needing little care. From my purple yam preserves I make jams, pies, mash… preserving purple yams was something I learned from my mother.

I was 3 when we fled to Nueva Vizcaya after Manila fell; I remember running… a neighbor hiding me because I was wearing a red dress which she said could be seen by special attack units. I remember the same neighbor losing her hearing after a bomb fell not far from where we were. I also remember a sword grazing my father's neck. I was very young and war is a terrible thing. But we were more fortunate than most. We had a pig which my father refused to give to drunk and marauding soldiers. It almost cost him his head. My pregnant mother ran all the way to the barracks, begging an officer to intervene and save her husband's life. He did, and in gratitude, she presented him with a spit-roasted pig. As for my older sister, my younger brother and me, we happily ate boiled purple yams for the next couple of years.

"Mama, is the *ube* ready?" asked Sophia.

"Not yet, we still have to let it cool," I said. *Ube halaya* is a little more labor intensive than plain purple yam preserves, requiring constant stirring (without overworking) to achieve a silky texture. Sophia likes it creamier than the recipe calls for.

"Mama," she continued, looking at me earnestly, "when I grow up, I will have the most beautiful wedding." I smiled. (Just the other day, she wanted to be an astronaut.) My Sophia, no matter the odds, will accept nothing but a bright future. *And why shouldn't you, dearest child. At your age, what dreams did I conjure? And what did my mother say? Your world, if my prayers have any weight, must be boundless, rose-colored... painless.*

Soon, I will need to replant more tubers. Grow them, gather them in. My purple yam looks even more vibrant in this light. This golden hour, just before sundown, makes everything a little clearer, less dispersed...unfading. And so we are emboldened. What extraordinary deeds shall we accomplish tomorrow? On this day, the year of our Lord, nineteen hundred and eighty three, no hero has yet fallen, no young women have yet been hanged, we are not yet exiled.

And that which we make may still endure.

Selected Essays

How a Manileña Learned a Language

THE BEARING WALL BORE A CRACK. A hairline gap that widened to a slit, through which our little secrets slithered and scattered. Out they came in a flurry of whispers, insistent and incoherent. For years, nobody could tell exactly what happened and why. What I do know is that my murdered pregnant great-aunt was 17, not 18, when strange men broke into the house. And if she did curse the place while the men were defiling her, she would have done so in the language of her foremothers: "Wǒ huì chánzhe nǐ." She would then have been a ghost with a grievance, roaming restlessly, rageful and relentless. As to why she stayed behind after Manila was declared an open city on December 26, 1941—I cannot say.

I can say, however, that the old stone house survived the war, and so did the rest of my family.

Another war would be fought decades later. The Philippines would fall under Martial Law, and almost every word would be deemed volatile and political. I was born during this time, and grew up learning to speak softly, mimicking the women in my family, with their silvery voices seemingly stripped of spite or spunk. I was about six years old when I noticed a crack on the wall. Whenever my elders held a finger to their lips cautioning that "the walls have ears," I would instinctively look for a long, thin line dividing an otherwise white and uninterrupted vertical space. I gathered that if walls could hear, then they must be privy to so many communicated thoughts; they must also be stalwart keepers of so many secrets. They sometimes crack, I reasoned, because secrets and thoughts can be so powerful and so forceful, they can strain even the strongest resisting body. I decided to learn the language of walls. Twenty years later, I painted them cameo pink, and then broke them in a poem.

"The Hay(na)ku of the Broken Fourth Wall" (initially titled "Manileñas"), was inspired by images and stories of growing up in a house supposedly haunted with a curse. Having lived with "ghosts," I had no desire to flesh them out. Instead, I had hoped to versify what I saw as fortified domestic spaces, and the lives lived within them. I wrote "Manileñas" in 1998, a year I devoted to poetry, while I was preparing to leave for the United States. I wanted to write a poem that would reflect how complex women's interior lives can be; I wanted to remember the sensibilities and thought processes that brought us thus far; and I wanted to have a sketch of scenes that were already vanishing before me.

In the U.S., my writing evolved under the mentorship of Remé Grefalda. Remé was unyielding. She drove me to a point where I was ready to scream, and I did. I called her my (tor)mentor, and she laughed, although not unkindly. I wish to point out that in Remé's world, everyone is important, because everyone has a story to tell. My poems and prose found their way into *Our Own Voice*, a literary ezine for the Filipino diaspora, which Remé founded. Also, through Remé, I came to know the poetry of Eileen Tabios. Eileen's poems are unlike anything I had ever encountered. I find them provocative, obviating language as I know it. I started paying more attention to postcolonial concerns in a multicultural setting; to the significance of decolonization, and the implications of being a diasporic writer drawing on cultural memory. At this point, I thought it fitting that "Manileñas," a poem I wrote as I was on the cusp of becoming an assimilated immigrant, should also metamorphose into a poetic form which reflects the "Filipino transcolonial experience." Hence, I re-arranged the lines according to the hay(na)ku form, a variant of haiku invented by Eileen Tabios. Traditionally comprised of one-, two-, and three-word lines, I find this form almost effortless (albeit, intentional in its effortlessness). And by "borrowing" a theatrical element, I was able to "break down" the metaphorical wall that figured so prominently in my childhood. Other than the form, and a few re-wordings to fit the new form, I left the original text largely intact. Although awkward in many places, "Manileñas" was my breakthrough poem for it gave me a voice during a time fraught with silence, in a language that was never truly my own.

Fortitude takes many forms. I write because of the women in my family. Untiring, enduring warriors and inventors of the language of walls, they always got the job done, no matter how mundane or how grueling. They taught me how to navigate and silently subvert those spaces that confine just as much as they fortify. And in the language of walls, this, too, is true Pinay grit. Having found my voice, I write from a place of gratitude. From the generosity of women, I learned an important secret—that everything is survivable, even silence.

The Hay(na)ku of the Broken Fourth Wall

—For my mother

Sand,
plaster, eggshell,
stone. Paint blisters,

painted
walls. Paint
over paint, rooftop

vine,
twin lettered
gate. Two girls

behind
walls that
were white and

then
blue and
then pink. Things

will
be added,
things will change,

and
it will
all be the

same.
Two births
in the midst

of
a raging
war, a ravaged

city
and white
walls that were

grimed
then ground.
Two breasts one

each
for a
suckling child, broken

down
pride and
bladder before the

bayonet,
buying and
selling for a

couple
of rice
cakes. Severed breasts

and
murdered children,
a weak nation

before
a weaker
one, and a

scattering
of enemies
looking for lives

to
blight, virgins
to suck, pigs

to
steal. Kisses
that wake sleeping

beauties,
sleep that
showers kisses for

deeper
sleep. Old
Manila after it

fell,
a river
to get dirty,

a
nation in
soot and grime,

in
debt, indebted.
Two wars to

brew,
one for
the future, one

for
the past.
Two little girls

in
twin frocks—
one with a

giggle,
one with
her pride. Nuns

and
a convent
school, a prayer

every
hour, rosary
beads and three

mysteries,
the first
Friday out. Little

girls
with rice
cakes and red

dresses,
looking for
their playground, huddled

with
homemade dolls,
one with a

rice
cake, one
with a bleeding

gum.
Heavy breasts
on stopped motherhood,

and
hungry knitting
in the hungry

dark.
Empty womb
and wasted milk

to
brew a
war, one for

the
future, one
for the past.

Waiting
on walls
that were white

and
then endless
restless waiting, for

something,
for a
dream, for a

man.
Piano keys
and red dresses

to
stop the
knitting in the

shallow
dark. (Piano
fingers tapping yellowed

keys,
sewing red
dresses, weaving water

dreams.
Lips that
mouth forever, hands

hammering
twin lettered
gates.) Old Manila

blowing
bubbles, dirty
cobbles, a river

rumbling
for the
first quarter storm.

Two
women raised
in a convent,

eyes
down on
mystery beads. Half

a
day in
the kitchen for

the
yellow green
leaves on the

floor,
for tomato
thoughts and pepper

talks,
for the
sun and their

place
at the
end of the

day.
Ysabel's yellowed
gown was white

with
lace and
ribbons and pearls

on
satin. There
were gossamer vows,

there
were uncolored
walls. Heavy breasts

on
late motherhood,
the pattern unlearned—

the
pattern of
blessings and curses

for
women loved
and bound. A

country
in chaos,
sandaled feet dirtied

on
the street,
deep hunger deeper

in
later years,
for babies born

in
war and
monsoon weather, like

Cecilia
and Ysabel,
like Ysabel's little

girls.
Walls that
were white and

then
blue, a
rooftop vine that

was
cut, and
twin letters on

a
gate that
stood for a

man.
Things were
added, things changed

and
then it
was all the

same.
Cecilia left
when she was

a
little old,
before the blue

walls,
the vase,
the pink walls.

Her
dreams were
love and little

girls,
and now
she is a

little
old, a
little old for

love
and little
girls. Ysabel stayed

for
the young
girls that were

hers,
her dreams
were water dreams,

warm
gloves on
piano fingers and

the
world in
a boat. Certainly

not
little girls,
certainly not growing

old.
Two women
falling in a

trap,
weaving water
dreams, waiting in

their
trap. Two
daughters, two wars

to
brew, one
for the future,

one
for the
past. *Sand, plaster,*

eggshell,
stone. Paint
blisters, painted walls.

Two
girls behind
walls that were

white
and then
blue and then

pink.
They stayed
when they were

young,
after they
were young, when

the
vines in
front were almost

at
rooftop and
the twin letters

on
the gate
stood for a

man.
Things were
added, things changed,

and
then it
was all the

same.
Red curtains
were taken down

and
white blinds
put up. Couch

covers
were taken
off and pastel

paints
shown off.
They built a

bar
and brought
it out, and

hung
paintings and
put them down,

or
hid them
(including the charcoal

sketch
of a
girl gazing at

coeurs
sacrés). The
tapestried peacocks are

gone,
the sculpted
horse is broken,

the
china set
untouched, and four

vases
now protect
the white inanimate

cat.
Two girls
to raise, not

unlike
Cecilia, not
unlike Ysabel. A

trap
of water
dreams for getting

out,
for lying
in. Endless, restless

waiting.
There is
madness in a

mother's
milk. Ysabel's
water dreams too

much
too late
for not so

perfect
little girls.
Brewed wars a

little
too strong.
Little girls a

little
too sweet.
Hidden thoughts turned

into
secrets into
shame. Rice cakes

and
red dresses
in the house

with
its sins,
waiting for the

girls
and the
walls that were

not
always pink.
Sand, plaster, eggshell.

The Color of Kalamunding

THERE IS NO GENTLENESS in the way I pick a fruit. I have committed all seven sins of memory, and it has left me short of breath and short of temper. I reach and yank, mercilessly, at clusters of kalamunding. I find it necessary in order to recapture fragmented perceptions of sweetness—to qualify what I remember of lemonades.

It is rather tiring, this business of separation. What does it matter if I break one branch off an eight-foot columnar tree? Will it really bother the roots? And what of the fruits when swiftly cut? Do the golden orange halves feel the loss of a golden orange whole? Is it really any worse than summer attempting to linger, unable to sustain its tilt toward the sun?

September, diplomatic September, is a truce between seasons, one refusing to leave, the other dragging its feet. The one that persists eventually withdraws. Its wake has left me with the most haunting of all failures of memory.

Withdrawal, according to my grandmother's nurse, is the beginning of separation. She could have painted it orange, for visual impact, and I still would have failed to acknowledge the process as death easing its way into and out of my grandmother's hallway.

It is an imposition, really, this business of dying on the dying. Suddenly, one finds one's self working around some invisible timetable. So many changes to get used to in a body that is, for all intents and purposes, no longer one's own.

Decreased food intake and increased sleep while alarming, failed to give me a sense perception of death. I refused it on my grandmother's account and behalf. She was 88 and mostly disoriented, but I chose to diagnose it as a temporary ailment that could respond to treatment. I really had no recourse but to grasp at life and providence, however fleeting; to prevent a fruit from falling, however ripe, if it meant the permanence of a season, or at least the prolonging of it.

Kalamunding lemonade, is still, in my opinion, the most refreshing of all summer drinks. An eight ounce glass normally requires two to three sliced fruits, juiced and diluted with water, and sugar, added to taste. It is a drink to toast past summers of citrusy sweetness, in the Manila of our half-remembered youths.

My grandmother's kalamunding tree has stood upright and cold-resistant in her California garden for nearly 40 years. Mature, striking, with oval-shaped leaves and fragrant, white flowers, it continues to bear hundreds of spherical, two-inch fruits year round.

The south part of the garden is a golden orange-evergreen landscape, perfect for gathering the thin, leathery rinds of an eternal present, to keep alive Filipino grandmothers and their not-quite-lime-not-quite-orange lemonades.

"It's okay not to eat," the hospice people explained.

At a certain point, food ceases to be a source of nourishment for the dying. If I had been more objective, I would have perceived my grandmother's gradual loss of appetite as symptomatic of a body preparing to die. Something more incorporeal was sustaining her, and had she been so inclined, she could have drawn a parchment-thin line between the physical material body she still inhabited, and the spiritual domain she was withdrawing to.

She preferred to sleep most of the time. I, however, opted to wake her up whenever I could. I wanted her reassurance that she wasn't dying yet, had hoped to glimpse the sprightly, kindly, beloved woman of my childhood. I spoke tenderly, as though words, my words, held power over life and death. But communication was becoming ineffectual. It would have been infinitely better had I silently held her hand through the night, for a few more nights, thereafter.

Persistence, being the most disquieting of all sins of memory, is the denial of one's own absolution. I am haunted by discrete moments of unconditional love. I would realize, years later, when her hold on life was already too tenuous, that I had very little time, very little chance for atonement.

She was picking at her bedding, talking about dead family members as though they were still alive. My grandmother, the caregiver says, "is losing her grounding to earth."

Two weeks prior to her death, her pulse beat and body temperature had begun fluctuating. Her skin was abnormally pale, her breathing, sharp, brisk. All I could do was help turn her to her side; put lotion on her thin, cold shins, on her thin, cold arms.

I write furiously of what I remember, for forgetfulness is a failure as terrible as persistence. How I long for the ability to flit between different moments in time, to kneel in place of my younger self.

Forgive me, for I will fail you. My love will be frail, and my will, frailer still.

On Monday, September 10th, I received a call from my cousin asking me to come immediately to my grandmother's house. I found my grandmother unresponsive, her eyes open, but unseeing. The next couple of days, we would be administering morphine every four hours. Her restlessness was increasing, her breathing, labored and erratic. I was never able to talk to her again.

I prayed. I read Kundera's *Immortality*, and decided I could never wave my arm with such freedom and grace. I gave it a try. I wandered around the house. I waited. I prayed.

My grandmother died on Thursday. "Surrounded by loved ones," as reported in the San Jose Mercury News. It seems so strange to find her in the obituaries. Surreal. How could it have been over so fast? What boundaries, what continuum, had she already crossed? Can she hear me, see me, love me still?

I never smelled candles. They say it is a common occurrence when someone close to you passes away. I did catch a whiff of something pleasant—an admixture of mangoes and jasmines—light, fragrant, ephemeral.

The coming weeks would bring changes. Mostly necessary. Some images, some scents, sounds, voices, instants have disappeared forever; some I try to grasp for longer than fractions of a second, to be bound and stored, and recalled for as long as I need them.

It has been seven months since we buried my grandmother. I was at her house the other day, to pick some kalamunding fruits. They were a sight to behold. Like little suns in the palm of my hand.

The house was a study in contrast. Too uncluttered. Too sparse. Somnolent, senescent. It used to hold more people than photographs, more food than remembered recipes. I suppose change is like that. The granddaughters have now become mothers. And my grandmother's daughters? They are now the same age as her when she was our young grandmother. I suppose some memories are like that, indelible.

There is a way to be gentle. Such as when I put my arms around my mother or my aunts. They are the not-quite-lime-not-quite-orange golden orange essence of my grandmother, and I, theirs. Maybe I will fail at failing them. I have suns in my hand.

This is a time for lemonades, for gathering seeds and flowers and leaves, and thin, leathery rinds. Find me a fruit, a round, ripe, radiant fruit hanging from an evergreen tree in an ever green garden, and I will pick it, ever so gently.

I would have wanted to end there. My life reading like a book, as though I have reached an epiphany of sorts. But as you must have surmised by now, I am perfectly flawed. I did mention in the beginning that I have committed all seven sins of memory. In the process of reconstruction, some memories have receded or never registered; others, blocked, misattributed, suggested, edited. For instance, the "whiff of something pleasant" could have been apples and orange blossoms, or an aromatic blend of herbs, but I somehow distinctly remember, although not with absolute precision, mangoes and jasmines, maybe because I have always associated these with my grandmother. In the forgetting curve, the world of fruits and flowers had never been more evanescent than at that point.

While I tried to be as objective as possible, my recollections are not faithful reproductions of my past. They are invariably colored by my experiences, my affects, by the imperfections and limitations of my own perceptions. There are myths in memory's truths.

I write to remember. Even when there are margins of error in my recounting. My memories of this specific time period —the events immediately preceding the death of my grandmother—could vary greatly from what my mother or any one of my aunts would recall. However, my memory's failures do not weaken my conscious recollections. They can never negate the magnitude of my pain or the depth of my love. As the psychologist Daniel L. Schacter explains, "the seven sins are an integral part of the mind's heritage because they are closely connected to features of memory which make it work well... They also illuminate how memory draws on the past to inform the present, preserves elements of present experience for future reference, and allows us to revisit the past at will."

I did reach an epiphany of sorts. There is a chance that I will choose to not be gentle with golden orange essences. You must have surmised how I am, by now. Not quite lime, not quite orange. In the world of fruits and flowers, I am excessively flawed. Such is my myth.

Find me an apple, a red, juicy apple.

Lost in Translation

I SPEAK TAGALOG PERFECTLY. And by Tagalog, I mean
the language used in 1930s Manila, which is now totally
archaic. Some examples are aklat/book, himlay/rest,
sapagkat/because — like I said, it's archaic and no one I
know really uses it anymore (except for the State of
California with its Tagalog forms and instructions which
even my mom couldn't understand so that she ends up
requesting the English version, anyway).

The Tagalog I grew up with more closely resembles what
is now known as "Filipino." Having said that, I very rarely
write in Filipino — the reason being, I'm not confident
enough to use it with sustained grace (and heaven forbid I
revert to Taglish! And by this, I mean the class-rooted 1980s
version). I did translate a poem by Albert Alejo from Filipino
to English, and another by Eileen Tabios from English to
Filipino. And regardless of the literary value (or lack of) of
my translated work, I find the practice and process absolutely
delightful—like putting together a challenging puzzle.

I decided to try Romaji next (this is the Westernized
version of Japanese writing, and the nearest I will
probably get to being remotely proficient in the language).
I started with the two haikus I wrote for *The Asahi Shimbun*
(although only the English versions were accepted and
published):

Eikō no keshiki, / Gorudengetoburijji / Natsu
Showa / 42

(Glorious scene / Golden Gate Bridge / Summer of / 67)

Sanfuranshisuko / Hagaki / Kanojo no kami no kin

(San Francisco / Postcard / Her golden hair)

While I can be as florid as I wish when translating into and from Tagalog/Filipino, with Japanese, I have to be the most concise that I can be (distilling each line into a single word, if possible), given that I neither have the command nor finesse required when translating any source text. (But that surely doesn't stop me from trying!)

My most recent attempt is a labor of love. I translated a verse from "For Paul"— my wedding poem—into Japanese, the only language, apart from English, that I have in common with my husband (and we're both truly terrible at it—but like I said, it's a labor of love). Some 10 hours later, this:

I will love you in the manner / of good wives, in the manner / of our grandmothers who walked / in faithfulness. I will stand / by you each day in the manner / of good men. I will lie down facing / you each night in the manner of hearts.

was shaped into this:

Ī tsuma no you ni / Watashi wa itoshi teru / Chūjitsu ni / Watashi wa aruku / Watashitachi no sobo no michi / Otoko no you ni / Otetsudai

shimasu / Mainichi / Maiban / Watashi wa anata
no tonari ni nemuru / Kokoro no you ni

*(Like a good wife / I love / Faithfully / I walk / Our
grandmothers' way / Like a (good) man / I support
you / Everyday / Every night / I sleep next to you /
Like a heart)*

I then asked someone who speaks Japanese at a native level
to edit, and this is what she came up with (with credit and
much gratitude to Gabri-san):

ii tsuma no you ni / watashi wa anata (w)o / aisuru
/ sobo-tachi no you ni / shinkou no michi (w)o /
issho ni ayumu. / zennin no you ni / mainichi,
soba de / shienshi-tsudzukeru / muki-au kokoro no
you ni / maiban / kao (w)o awasenagara / soba
de nemuru

*(In the manner of good wives / I will love you / In
the manner of our grandmothers / I will walk the
path of faith with you / In the manner of good men
(people) / Everyday, by your side, I will continue
to support you / In the manner of hearts that face
towards one another / Every night, while facing
you, / I will sleep by your side)*

which is the version most closely resembling the original
poem. To make it more cadenced, I tweaked it to read:

ii tsuma no you ni / watashi wa anata aisuru / sobo-tachi no you ni / shinkou no michi wo issho ni ayumu / Meiyo aru hito no you ni / mainichi, soba de shienshi-tsudzukeru / maiban kao wo awasenagara / Hata de nemuru / Kokoro no you ni

(Like a good wife / I love you / Like our grandmothers / I walk the path of faith / Like honorable men / Everyday, I support you / Every night, I face you / Sleep beside you / Like a heart)

(Okay, so perhaps Gabri's version is best.)

And why do translations matter? Because language is fluid, and it is one way to ensure that written texts survive. A thousand years from now, when everything I know has either evolved or eroded, I would like to think that my love still lives, battle-worn and heartstrong.

Traveling with Tsinelas

SOME DAYS, IF I SQUINT MY EYES, JUST SO, there she will be, my Manila. Sailing past San Francisco, in the middle of New York City, or on a corner of London Town. Then all too briefly, she is gone, lineaments concealed, edges tucked away.

An expatriate friend of mine once said that we carry our home in our hearts wherever we go. And so, I carry with me, wherever I go, a pair of slippers. The easier to slip into, the more I like it. This tradition started twenty years ago when, while traveling alone in Europe, I was invited to a Filipino family's home for dinner. At the time, it had been more than three months since I laid eyes on a fellow Pinoy or tasted Filipino food. Imagine my excitement when, through the glass front door, I glimpsed a row of pairs of *tsinelas* lining the entryway. It was the most beautiful sight. They stood for everything I was so sorely and terribly missing—my home, my family, fragments of my culture.

Philippine slippers, traditionally in the form of wooden clogs or *bakya*, are said to date as far back as precolonial times; I prefer to think of them as humble bearers of the rough maps of our people's noblest quests. Thus, for the last two decades, I have been traveling with tsinelas, for what other token of my being Pinay is more practical, more convenient and more tangible?

Tokens aside, nothing, of course, beats the real thing—my homeland in all her sultry, jangling, ragged, luscious, cerulean, burnt amber, ironic, contradictory, heartbreakingly proud, and heartbreakingly lovely glory. In the most hushed hours of my day, I think of her. Then I am home, more often than she knows.

Lolo Claudio in Colorado

IF A POET WERE MEASURED BY HER METERS,
does she mark out the ground where she broke her stride?
The miles I've logged to get here are strewn with poetic
intentions. I came to America with a luggage overpacked
with poems, and at San Francisco Airport, I collapsed my
images into one overwhelming thought: I could be a poet
here. But one thing I learned about poetry and America is
that they are both not for the faint-hearted.

A few years ago, a hundred-year-old photograph came to
mind. It framed a poem I included in a manuscript that was
published in 2010. The poem, "Lolo Claudio in Colorado," is an
American love story, and had it ended more happily, I wouldn't
be here at all. As it happens, I lived to write the poem.

In the 1900s, Filipinos, being U.S. nationals, were allowed
to travel freely to America. Perhaps it was the pursuit of
happiness, or the promise of "unalienable rights," or both,
that prompted many young men, my great-grandfather
included, to pack their trunks and embark on a voyage across
the Pacific. My great-grandfather settled in Colorado
between 1905 and 1910. Sometime during that period, he fell
in love. Lolo Claudio didn't take matters of the heart, or of
freedom, lightly. At 12 years old, he witnessed the execution
of Jose Rizal. Even then, he understood that love and liberty,
for many people, came at a cost. And in America in 1910, he
found out that one couldn't simply marry whom one loved.
There were laws that prohibited this, both constitutional and

cultural. But if one were not free to love, he told himself, one wasn't free at all.

He decided to go back to the Philippines and, like other young men, found a job, bought a house, got married, and raised a family. He lived to be almost a hundred, surviving his wife and many of his friends. In moments when he was alone with great-grandchildren he believed to be too young to understand, he would pull out of his wallet a very old photograph, and trace with his finger the image of a beautiful girl. "It was too cold in Colorado," he would simply say.

His eldest child, my grandfather, moved to the U.S. in the 1970s during the early years of Martial Law. He and his wife and children settled in the San Francisco Bay Area; my mother, who was already married at the time, fell under the third preference of the family preference immigrant visas, and had to wait a few more years to be given a "green card." I would grow up in a society with enforced martial rule, on the one hand, and the promise of freedom in America, on the other. My pre-immigrant images of America, formed by my U.S.-based relatives, included Jimmy Carter and Ronald Reagan juxtaposed with Lawrence Welk. For my grandparents (and my parents, eventually), adapting to a whole new sociopolitical and cultural system meant being one step closer to the American Dream. When I think of a great American love story, I think of my elders and all the other *manongs*, whose heritage I share, ploughing America's unyielding furrows. Turning over the earth meant, for them, giving their children the right to call this place home.

There are more than three million Filipino Americans scattered across the U.S. today, and nearly 500,000 call the San Francisco Bay Area home. Demographically, we make up more than one percent of the population—and theoretically, we have enough signatures to qualify a measure for a ballot, more than enough people to make a city, more than enough strides to change the future.

I am a poet based in the San Francisco Bay Area. How can I not be moved by shorelines, or by ground built on rubble and traversed by many faults? I wrestle with the weight of words. At the corner of San Francisco's Kearny and Jackson, the grand old men still stand watch; and in Santa Clara County, there is a place that leaves the light on for me. Take me home on a rail, from the southern base to the northern tip of a peninsula. The measure of a poet's stride equals a bridge.

ACKNOWLEDGMENTS

"From 'The Enormous River Encircling the World'" was first published in *Galatea Resurrects*, April 2017.

"Isle of Skye, 1920" was first published in *Moss Trill*, September 2017.

"Point Joe" was first published in *Our Own Voice*, April 2012.

"Tea in the Sahara" was first published in *Marsh Hawk Review*, March 2011.

"The Short Season Between Two Silences" was first published in *Moria Poetry*, Fall 2010/Winter 2011.

"A Day at the Museum with a Poet" appeared in *Marsh Hawk Review (Fall 2018)* edited by Eileen R. Tabios.

"The Cabinet of the World and the Journeys of Women" appeared in *Marsh Hawk Review (Fall 2018)* edited by Eileen R. Tabios. Quote from Margaret Kemp's "Caroline and the Knowledge of the World." Poem inspired by the "Enchanted Palace" Exhibition (London, 2010), and by "Wunderkammer" (Royal Collection Trust).

"Last word is the poet's calling" was first published by Open Palm Press in April 2010 as part of a fundraiser for Haiti.

"The Auction" was crafted for the Books on Chairs Project, February 2013.

"In the Island of Good Boots" was first published in *Galatea Resurrects 2017* in response to Alex Tizon's article, "My Family Slave" as regards Eudocia Tomas Pulido.

"B&O Blues No. 3" was first published by Locofo Chaps, March 2017. Additional reference from the Harvard University Library Open Collections Program, Immigration to the United States, 1789-1930.

"San Francisco Haiku" was first published in *The Asahi Shimbun*, September 2017.

"The Summer of Love" was first published in *Migo Zine* Issue 1. Quote on page 4 is by Nicholas von Hoffman. Illustrated by Aileen Cassinetto.

"The Art of Salamat" was first published by Locofo Chaps, April 2017. Additional reference from the Senate of the Philippines, 17th Congress, July 2011.

"The Boatman's Book Spine Poetry" was featured in the "Chromatext Rebooted" Exhibit, Cultural Center of the Philippines, November 2015 to January 2016. "The Boatman's Book Spine Poetry" is inspired by titles featured in *Our Own Voice's* Bookshelf. Featured authors include Patria Rivera, Eileen R. Tabios, Remé Grefalda, Luis H. Francia, Angela Narciso Torres, Gemino H. Abad, Rey Ventura, Jon Pineda, Lysley Tenorio, Aimee Nezhukumatathil, Jose Y. Dalisay Jr., Angelo R. Lacuesta, Luisa A. Igloria, Rick Barot, Ivy Alvarez, and Alfred A. Yuson.

"Salambao" first appeared in the Harford Poetry and Literary Society's annual publication, *Manorborn*, in 2009.

"Rooted" was first published in *Marsh Hawk Review*, Fall 2016.

"Orange Jessamine Road" was first published in *Our Own Voice*, April 2012.

"How a Manileña Learned a Language" was first published in *Our Own Voice*, January 2015.

"The Hay(na)ku of the Broken Fourth Wall" previously appeared in *Traje de Boda* (Meritage Press, 2010). Its original form was completed in 1998.

"The Color of Kalamunding" was previously published in *Our Own Voice*, August 2009.

"Lost in Translation" was first published in *Medium*, October 2017. Japanese translation by Gabrielle Reinecke.

"Traveling with Tsinelas" first appeared in the anthology *Hanggang sa Muli*, published by Tahanan Books in 2012.

Lolo Claudio in Colorado was first published in *Positively Filipino*, July 2014.

CPSIA information can be obtained
at www.ICGtesting.com
Printed in the USA
FSHW010514071218
54301FS